Be Mine

ISBN 978-1-63575-356-1 (Paperback)
ISBN 978-1-63525-617-8 (Hard Cover)
ISBN 978-1-63525-618-5 (Digital)

Copyright © 2017 by Pamela Berry

All rights reserved. No part of this publication may be reproduced, distributed, or transmitted in any form or by any means, including photocopying, recording, or other electronic or mechanical methods without the prior written permission of the publisher. For permission requests, solicit the publisher via the address below.

Christian Faith Publishing, Inc.
296 Chestnut Street
Meadville, PA 16335
www.christianfaithpublishing.com

Printed in the United States of America

Pamela Berry

Andrea

I would like to dedicate this book in honor of my loving little sister. She freely gives her time and her love each and every day. Her light shines bright all along her way of life. She is like a precious, priceless, and genuine jewel. Her love and laughter give her a great personality, and her attitude can be seen in the smile that she wears. Whenever she goes anywhere, she always thinks of me. I thank God for that loving little sister of mine. She is there for me, and I am there for her. It is amazing to know that she lives to give, and I would not trade her for anything in this world. Through thick and thin, we are forever sisters to the end, and love is through it all.

Love ya,
Pamela

There once was a young girl named Susanne Quin Morann. Her parents taught her to love and to do all that she can. She grew up in a small country place and always had a big smile on her face.

Susanne thought of everyone and everything. On bad days, she thought of good songs to sing. Friendly and kind, her friends stayed on her mind.

Susanne believed in the truth, and she told it as well. If lies were spoken, it would ring her bell. From day to day, prayer was her way.

Five days a week, Susanne went to school. She learned many things and followed the rule. Over all of the rest, science was her best.

Susanne was quick to do her work, quick to study, and quick to sit with her buddy. She loved her teacher, and to be in her class. It was like the flowers that come from the grass.

Lessons that we learn are like gifts that we show. They stay in our minds, and they help us to grow. From beginning to end, books are your friend.

On Saturdays, Susanne liked to stay home, to be with her dog, and to talk on the phone. She loved her dog, and he loved her too.

That love is why she decided to work with animal rescue. The animals were filled with lots of love and needed much care. Between Susanne and the dogs, there was no room to spare.

Time went by and was spent in a very special way. Susanne got what she gave to the dogs each and every day. Anyone could see it was a job meant to be.

On Sundays, the family went to the house of God. They were joined by others, and all were like peas in a pod. It was a special place to find God's grace.

All took a look in His great book. They learned how to live and how much to give. Faith, hope, and love were spread as the truth was read.

Everyone understood that Jesus came to seek and to save; He was a friend to all, and to all He gave. He lived his life, He never lied, He was mistreated, but for all He died. After He died some people cried, but that was not the end, my friend.

He rose from the grave to show that His Father does save. He did everything in the name of love, and He watches us from heaven above. Susanne said, "Because He lives I know that He gives."

She went home and knew she was not alone. Her love for Him had really grown. Susanne had a great life for a great reason.

Jesus was her friend through every season. He was happy to stay and to help her each day. He lived in her heart, and never would He depart.

There was no need to fear because Jesus was near. Susanne would say to always trust and obey.

She held on to the promises that Jesus said. They were in the Bible, and they were written in red. Promises from above are treasures of love.

Jesus wants to share His promises with you, to help get you through, and be your friend too. Three little letters are simple but true. The best way for me is to follow *A B C*.

Ask Him to forgive you for what you have done wrong. Believe in His Word, and you will be strong. Confess to Jesus all of the bad things that you do, and remember how much Jesus loves you.

He will come live in your heart and give you a fresh start. You will live to give love that sticks like glue, and you will have a great life just like your friend Susanne Q.

About the Author

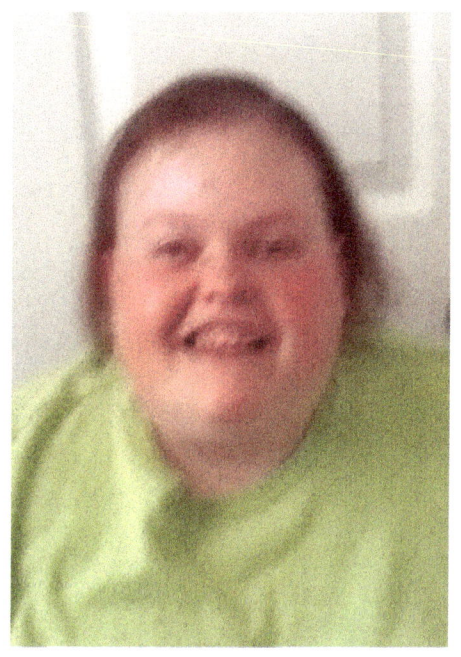

My name is Pamela Berry, and I was born in 1982. I grew up in a small town in North Carolina and was raised in a Christian home. My family and I attended church on a regular basis, but I was still the average child. You could say that I was full of myself and such a mess. I had everyday problems, with mother's hand to guide me. As I got older, it seems like the problems got bigger. When I was sixteen years old, I was diagnosed with brain cancer. It was a long and hard road, but in August of 2000, I was cancer-free. In December of 2001, I had a massive stroke. Doctors told my family that I would not come out alive. Thanks to God and the loving prayers, I did come out and survived. I still have other problems that handicapped me in certain ways. I am legally blind, I have loss of hearing, and I do not have as much mobility as I once had. I live from day to day because we are never promised tomorrow. When I face trials and problems in my life today, I hold on to God's great promises of love. People ask me how I can smile after all I have been through. I tell them it is all because of God's amazing grace. I am a Christian who stands on the solid Rock, and I freely share the love that He gives to me.